BACKYARD WILDLIFE

Raccoons

by Emily Green

BELLWETHER MEDIA • MINNEAPOLIS, MN

Note to Librarians, Teachers, and Parents:

Blastoff! Readers are carefully developed by literacy experts and combine standards-based content with developmentally appropriate text.

Level 1 provides the most support through repetition of high-frequency words, light text, predictable sentence patterns, and strong visual support.

Level 2 offers early readers a bit more challenge through varied simple sentences, increased text load, and less repetition of high-frequency words.

Level 3 advances early-fluent readers toward fluency through increased text and concept load, less reliance on visuals, longer sentences, and more literary language.

Level 4 builds reading stamina by providing more text per page, increased use of punctuation, greater variation in sentence patterns, and increasingly challenging vocabulary.

Level 5 encourages children to move from "learning to read" to "reading to learn" by providing even more text, varied writing styles, and less familiar topics.

Whichever book is right for your reader, Blastoff! Readers are the perfect books to build confidence and encourage a love of reading that will last a lifetime!

This edition first published in 2011 by Bellwether Media, Inc.

No part of this publication may be reproduced in whole or in part without written permission of the publisher. For information regarding permission, write to Bellwether Media, Inc., Attention: Permissions Department, 5357 Penn Avenue South, Minneapolis, MN 55419.

Library of Congress Cataloging-in-Publication Data
Green, Emily K., 1966–
    Raccoons / by Emily Green.
      p. cm. – (Blastoff! readers: Backyard wildlife)
    Includes bibliographical references and index.
    Summary: "Developed by literacy experts for students in kindergarten through grade three, this book introduces raccoons to young readers through leveled text and related photos"–Provided by publisher.
    ISBN 978-1-60014-444-8 (hardcover : alk. paper)
    1. Raccoon—Juvenile literature. I. Title.
    QL737.C26G74 2010
    599.76'32–dc22
                                                         2010006434

Printed in the United States of America, North Mankato, MN.
080110   1162

Contents

Raccoons are furry animals with long, bushy tails. Their tails have stripes.

Black fur circles
a raccoon's
eyes like a mask.
This helps a
raccoon see
at night.

Raccoons sleep
during the day.
They hunt for
food at night.

Raccoons have sharp **claws** on their paws. Claws help raccoons climb trees.

Raccoons are **scavengers**. They gather food wherever they can find it.

Raccoons eat
fruits, nuts,
insects, and
small animals.
They even steal
eggs from nests!

Some raccoons dip their food in water. They also pick off parts they do not want to eat.

Raccoons live
in cities, forests,
and farmlands.

Some raccoons use their paws to open trash cans. They hope to find a tasty meal!

Glossary

claws—sharp, curved nails at the ends of an animal's fingers and toes

insects—small animals with six legs and hard outer bodies; insect bodies are divided into three parts.

scavengers—animals that gather and eat food wherever they can find it; scavengers often look for food in trash cans.

To Learn More

AT THE LIBRARY

Arnosky, Jim. *Raccoon On His Own*. New York, N.Y.: G.P. Putnam's, 2001.

Fowler, Allan. *Raccoons*. New York, N.Y.: Children's Press, 2000.

Swanson, Diane. *Welcome to the World of Raccoons*. Milwaukee, Wisc.: Gareth Stevens, 1998.

ON THE WEB

Learning more about raccoons is as easy as 1, 2, 3.

1. Go to www.factsurfer.com.

2. Enter "raccoons" into the search box.

3. Click the "Surf" button and you will see a list of related Web sites.

With factsurfer.com, finding more information is just a click away.

Index

The images in this book are reproduced through the courtesy of: Denise Kappa, front cover; Bill Draker/
Photolibrary, p. 5; Ryan M. Bolton, p. 7; Peter Wey, p. 9; Juniors Bildarchiv/Age Fotostock, p. 11; Juan
Martinez, pp. 13, 15 (left), 19 (middle); Dwight Kuhn/Dwight Kuhn Photography, p. 15; Geanina Bechea,
p. 15 (middle); Romanchuck Dimitry, p. 15 (right); Peter Weimann/Photolibrary, p. 17; Jeff Grabert, p. 19;
S. Borisov, p. 19 (left); Mika Heittola, p. 19 (right); Corbis/Photolibrary, p. 21.